My Magical Brown Unicorn

Reading Comprehension Journal For Kids

Created By
Ren Lowe

How To Use This Journal

Use This Journal **While** you are reading
OR
After you have completed reading a book
to help you remember key details

Feel free to Color, Draw, and Write in your Journal

There Is No Wrong Way!

Easy enough for kids to use by themselves
or
With an Adult

Remember
To…....

HAVE FUN!!!!

Copyright © 2020 Ren Lowe

All rights reserved. This book or any portion thereof may not be reproduced or used in any manner whatsoever without the express written permission of the publisher except for the use of brief quotations in a book review

Publisher: Royaltee Press LLC

ISBN: 978-1-7359437-1-8

Published and Printed in The United States of America

www.royalteepress.com

THIS JOURNAL BELONGS TO:

Date.. / /

Whimsical Words

What New Words Will You Discover While Reading?
Write Them In The Unicorn Below

Date.. / /

The Title Of My Book Is _____

The Author Is _____

Look At The Cover Of The Book What Do You Think This Book Is About? _____
_____
_____

1. Is This Story Fiction Or Non-Fiction? _____
_____

2. Could This Story Really Happen? _____
_____

3. What Is Your Favorite Part? Why? _____
_____
_____
_____

4. Do You Like The Story? _____ Why Or Why Not? _____
_____
_____

What Would You Do If You Were In The Story
_____
_____
_____

Date.. / /

This book makes me feel

Who are the characters?

1. _____
2. _____
3. _____
4. _____

Is there a problem?
Write About it

_____
_____
_____
_____

What happens at the...

Beginning of the story
Draw Or Write About it

Middle of the story
Draw Or Write About it

Ending of the story
Draw Or Write About it

Date.. / /

TODAY I READ ABOUT...
WRITE ABOUT IT, DRAW ABOUT IT, OR DO BOTH

_____

_____
_____
_____
_____
_____
_____

Date.. / /

Whimsical Words

What New Words Will You Discover While Reading?
Write Them In The Unicorn Below

Date.. / /

The Title Of My Book Is _____

The Author Is _____

Look At The Cover Of The Book What Do You Think This Book Is About? _____
_____
_____

1. Is This Story Fiction Or Non-Fiction? _____
_____

2. Could This Story Really Happen? _____
_____

3. What Is Your Favorite Part?   Why? _____
_____
_____
_____

4. Do You Like The Story? _____ Why Or Why Not? _____
_____
_____

 What Would You Do If You Were In The Story
_____
_____
_____

Date.. / /

THIS BOOK MAKES ME FEEL

WHO ARE THE CHARACTERS?

1. _____
2. _____
3. _____
4. _____

IS THERE A PROBLEM?
Write About it

_____
_____
_____
_____

WHAT HAPPENS AT THE...

BEGINNING OF THE STORY
Draw Or Write About it

MIDDLE OF THE STORY
Draw Or Write About it

ENDING OF THE STORY
Draw Or Write About it

Date.. / /

TODAY I READ ABOUT...
WRITE ABOUT IT, DRAW ABOUT IT, OR DO BOTH

_____

_____

_____

_____

_____

_____

_____

Date.. / /

Whimsical Words

What New Words Will You Discover While Reading?
Write Them In The Unicorn Below

Date.. / /

The Title Of My Book Is _____

The Author Is _____

Look At The Cover Of The Book What Do You Think This Book Is About? _____
_____
_____

1. Is This Story Fiction Or Non-Fiction? _____
_____

2. Could This Story Really Happen? _____
_____

3. What Is Your Favorite Part? Why? _____
_____
_____
_____

4. Do You Like The Story? _____ Why Or Why Not? _____
_____

 What Would You Do If You Were In The Story
_____
_____
_____

Date.. / /

THIS BOOK MAKES ME FEEL

WHO ARE THE CHARACTERS?

1. _____
2. _____
3. _____
4. _____

IS THERE A PROBLEM?
Write About it

_____
_____
_____
_____

WHAT HAPPENS AT THE...

BEGINNING OF THE STORY
Draw Or Write About it

MIDDLE OF THE STORY
Draw Or Write About it

ENDING OF THE STORY
Draw Or Write About it

Date.. / /

TODAY I READ ABOUT...
WRITE ABOUT IT, DRAW ABOUT IT, OR DO BOTH

_____

_____

_____

_____

_____

_____

_____

Date.. / /

Whimsical Words

What New Words Will You Discover While Reading?
Write Them In The Unicorn Below

Date.. / /

The Title Of My Book Is _____

The Author Is _____

Look At The Cover Of The Book What Do You Think This Book Is About? _____
_____
_____

1. Is This Story Fiction Or Non-Fiction? _____
_____

2. Could This Story Really Happen? _____
_____

3. What Is Your Favorite Part? Why? _____
_____
_____
_____

4. Do You Like The Story? _____ Why Or Why Not? _____
_____
_____

What Would You Do If You Were In The Story
_____
_____
_____

Date.. / /

This Book Makes Me Feel

Who are the Characters?

1. _____
2. _____
3. _____
4. _____

Is There a Problem?
Write About it

_____
_____
_____
_____

What Happens at the...

Beginning of the Story

Draw Or Write About it

Middle of the Story

Draw Or Write About it

Ending of the Story

Draw Or Write About it

Date.. / /

TODAY I READ ABOUT...
WRITE ABOUT IT, DRAW ABOUT IT, OR DO BOTH

_____

_____

_____

_____

_____

_____

_____

Date.. / /

Whimsical Words

What New Words Will You Discover While Reading?
Write Them In The Unicorn Below

Date.. / /

The Title Of My Book Is _____

The Author Is _____

Look At The Cover Of The Book What Do You Think This Book Is About? _____
_____
_____

1. Is This Story Fiction Or Non-Fiction? _____
_____

2. Could This Story Really Happen? _____
_____

3. What Is Your Favorite Part?   Why? _____
_____
_____
_____

4. Do You Like The Story? _____ Why Or Why Not? _____
_____
_____

What Would You Do If You Were In The Story
_____
_____
_____

Date.. / /

This book makes me feel

Who are the characters?

1. _____
2. _____
3. _____
4. _____

Is there a problem?
Write About it

_____
_____
_____
_____

What happens at the...

Beginning of the story

Draw Or Write About it

Middle of the story

Draw Or Write About it

Ending of the story

Draw Or Write About it

Date.. / /

TODAY I READ ABOUT...
WRITE ABOUT IT, DRAW ABOUT IT, OR DO BOTH

Date.. / /

Whimsical Words

What New Words Will You Discover While Reading? Write Them In The Unicorn Below

Date.. / /

The Title Of My Book Is _____

The Author Is _____

Look At The Cover Of The Book What Do You Think This Book Is About? _____
_____
_____

1. Is This Story Fiction Or Non-Fiction? _____
_____

2. Could This Story Really Happen? _____
_____

3. What Is Your Favorite Part? Why? _____
_____
_____
_____

4. Do You Like The Story? _____ Why Or Why Not? _____
_____

 What Would You Do If You Were In The Story
_____
_____
_____

Date.. / /

This book makes me feel

Who are the characters?

1. _____
2. _____
3. _____
4. _____

Is there a problem?
Write About it

What happens at the...

Beginning of the story
Draw Or Write About it

Middle of the story
Draw Or Write About it

Ending of the story
Draw Or Write About it

Date.. / /

TODAY I READ ABOUT...

WRITE ABOUT IT, DRAW ABOUT IT, OR DO BOTH

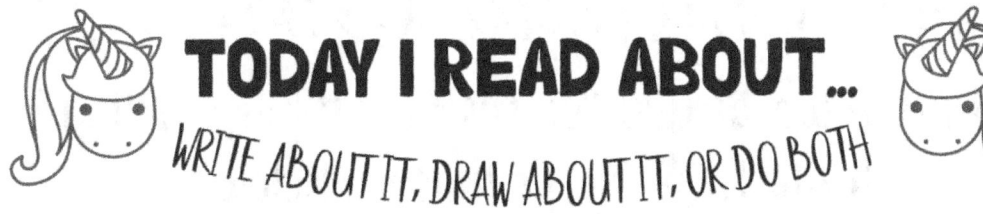

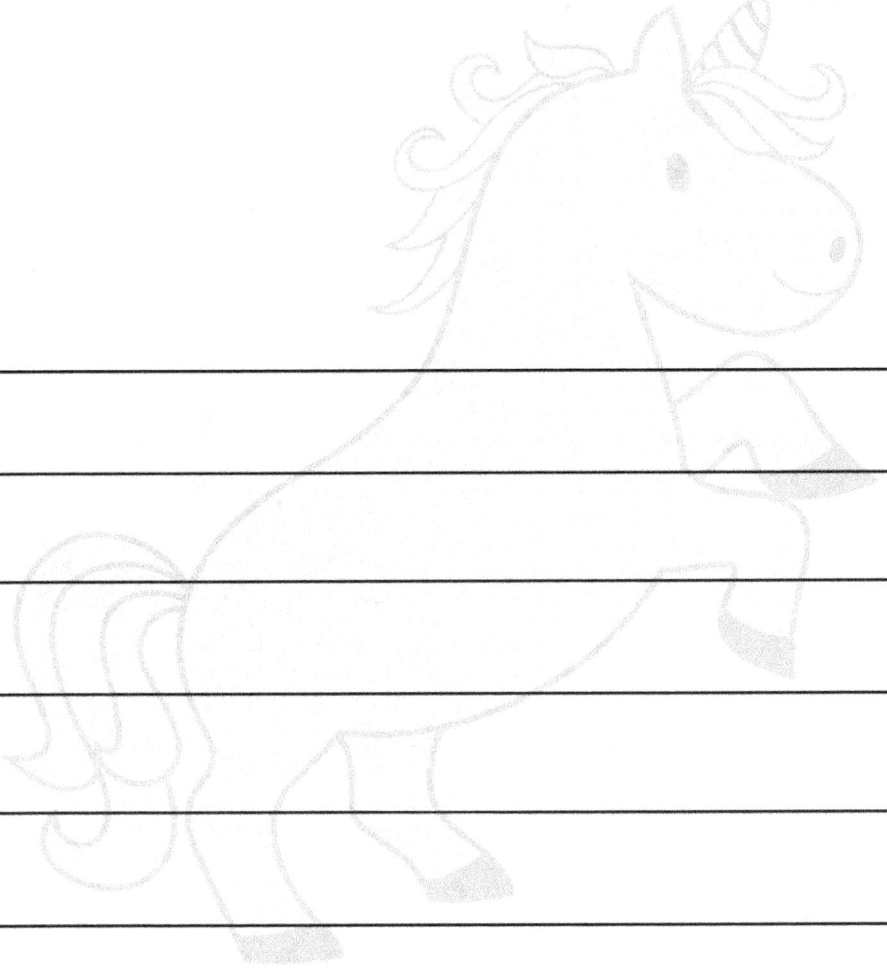

Date.. / /

Whimsical Words

What New Words Will You Discover While Reading? Write Them In The Unicorn Below

Date.. / /

The Title Of My Book Is _____

The Author Is _____

Look At The Cover Of The Book What Do You Think This Book Is About? _____
_____
_____

1. Is This Story Fiction Or Non-Fiction? _____
_____

2. Could This Story Really Happen? _____
_____

3. What Is Your Favorite Part? Why? _____
_____
_____
_____

4. Do You Like The Story? _____ Why Or Why Not? _____
_____

 What Would You Do If You Were In The Story
_____
_____
_____

Date.. / /

This book makes me feel

Who are the characters?

1. _____
2. _____
3. _____
4. _____

Is there a problem?
Write About it

_____
_____
_____
_____

What happens at the...

Beginning of the story
Draw Or Write About it

Middle of the story
Draw Or Write About it

Ending of the story
Draw Or Write About it

Date.. / /

TODAY I READ ABOUT...
WRITE ABOUT IT, DRAW ABOUT IT, OR DO BOTH

_____

_____

_____

_____

_____

_____

_____

Date.. / /

Whimsical Words

What New Words Will You Discover While Reading?
Write Them In The Unicorn Below

Date.. / /

The Title Of My Book Is _____

The Author Is _____

Look At The Cover Of The Book What Do You Think This Book Is About? _____
_____
_____

1. Is This Story Fiction Or Non-Fiction? _____
_____

2. Could This Story Really Happen? _____
_____

3. What Is Your Favorite Part? Why? _____
_____
_____
_____

4. Do You Like The Story? _____ Why Or Why Not? _____
_____
_____

What Would You Do If You Were In The Story
_____
_____
_____

Date.. / /

This book makes me feel

Who are the characters?

1. _____
2. _____
3. _____
4. _____

Is there a problem?
Write About it

_____
_____
_____
_____

What happens at the...

Beginning of the story
Draw Or Write About it

Middle of the story
Draw Or Write About it

Ending of the story
Draw Or Write About it

Date.. / /

TODAY I READ ABOUT...
WRITE ABOUT IT, DRAW ABOUT IT, OR DO BOTH

_____

_____

_____

_____

_____

_____

_____

Date.. / /

Whimsical Words

What New Words Will You Discover While Reading?
Write Them In The Unicorn Below

Date.. / /

The Title Of My Book Is _____

The Author Is _____

Look At The Cover Of The Book What Do You Think This Book Is About? _____
_____
_____

1. Is This Story Fiction Or Non-Fiction? _____
_____

2. Could This Story Really Happen? _____
_____

3. What Is Your Favorite Part? Why? _____
_____
_____
_____

4. Do You Like The Story? _____ Why Or Why Not? _____
_____
_____

What Would You Do If You Were In The Story
_____
_____
_____

Date.. / /

THIS BOOK MAKES ME FEEL

WHO ARE THE CHARACTERS?

1. _____
2. _____
3. _____
4. _____

IS THERE A PROBLEM?
Write About it

_____
_____
_____
_____

WHAT HAPPENS AT THE...

BEGINNING OF THE STORY
Draw Or Write About it

MIDDLE OF THE STORY
Draw Or Write About it

ENDING OF THE STORY
Draw Or Write About it

Date.. / /

TODAY I READ ABOUT...

WRITE ABOUT IT, DRAW ABOUT IT, OR DO BOTH

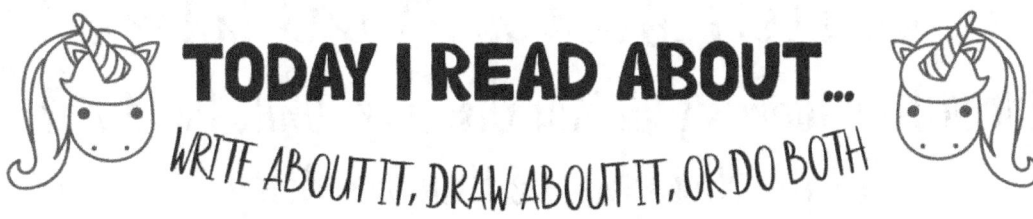

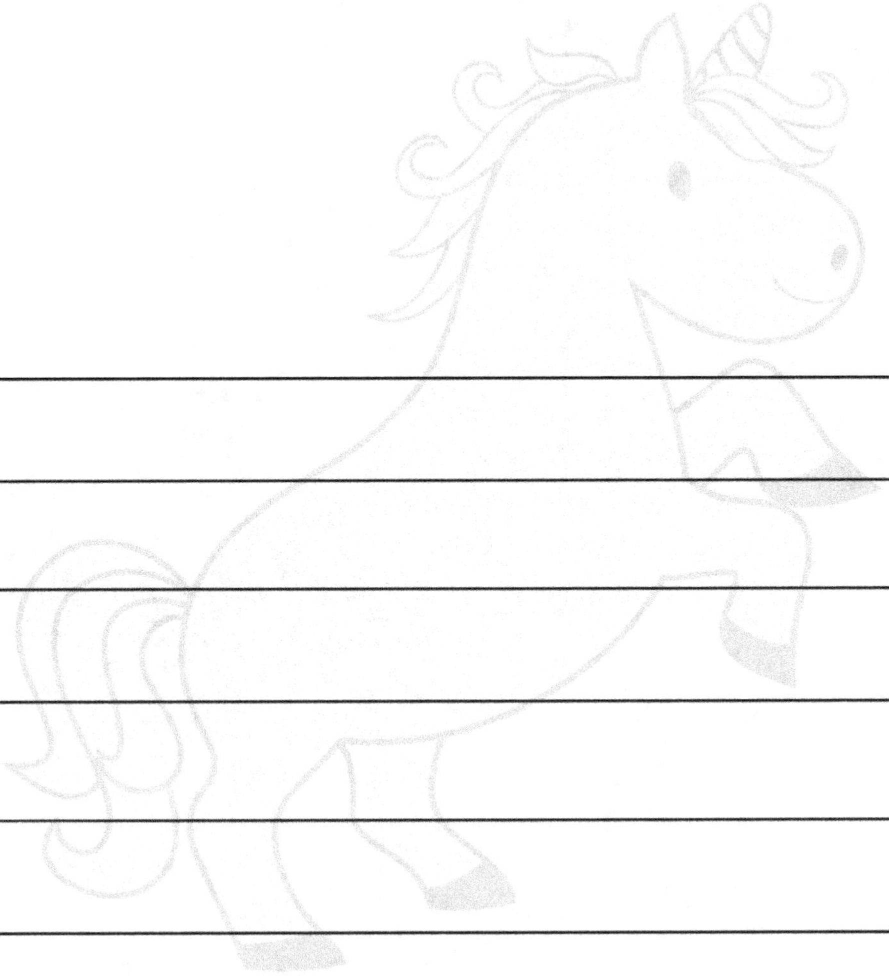

Date.. / /

Whimsical Words

What New Words Will You Discover While Reading? Write Them In The Unicorn Below

Date.. / /

The Title Of My Book Is _____

The Author Is _____

Look At The Cover Of The Book What Do You Think This Book Is About? _____
_____
_____

1. Is This Story Fiction Or Non-Fiction? _____
_____

2. Could This Story Really Happen? _____
_____

3. What Is Your Favorite Part? Why? _____
_____
_____

4. Do You Like The Story? _____ Why Or Why Not? _____
_____

What Would You Do If You Were In The Story
_____
_____
_____

Date.. / /

THIS BOOK MAKES ME FEEL

WHO ARE THE CHARACTERS?

1. _____
2. _____
3. _____
4. _____

IS THERE A PROBLEM?
Write About it

_____
_____
_____
_____

WHAT HAPPENS AT THE...

BEGINNING OF THE STORY
Draw Or Write About it

MIDDLE OF THE STORY
Draw Or Write About it

ENDING OF THE STORY
Draw Or Write About it

Date.. / /

TODAY I READ ABOUT...
WRITE ABOUT IT, DRAW ABOUT IT, OR DO BOTH

_____

_____

_____

_____

_____

_____

_____

Date.. / /

Whimsical Words

What New Words Will You Discover While Reading?
Write Them In The Unicorn Below

Date.. / /

The Title Of My Book Is _____

The Author Is _____

Look At The Cover Of The Book What Do You Think This Book Is About? _____
_____
_____

1. Is This Story Fiction Or Non-Fiction? _____
_____

2. Could This Story Really Happen? _____
_____

3. What Is Your Favorite Part? Why? _____
_____
_____
_____

4. Do You Like The Story? _____ Why Or Why Not? _____
_____
_____

What Would You Do If You Were In The Story
_____
_____
_____

Date.. / /

THIS BOOK MAKES ME FEEL

WHO ARE THE CHARACTERS?

1. _____
2. _____
3. _____
4. _____

IS THERE A PROBLEM?
Write About it

_____
_____
_____

WHAT HAPPENS AT THE...

BEGINNING OF THE STORY
Draw Or Write About it

MIDDLE OF THE STORY
Draw Or Write About it

ENDING OF THE STORY
Draw Or Write About it

Date.. / /

TODAY I READ ABOUT...
WRITE ABOUT IT, DRAW ABOUT IT, OR DO BOTH

_____

_____

_____

_____

_____

_____

_____

Date.. / /

Whimsical Words

What New Words Will You Discover While Reading?
Write Them In The Unicorn Below

Date.. / /

The Title Of My Book Is _____

The Author Is _____

Look At The Cover Of The Book What Do You Think This Book Is About? _____
_____
_____

1. Is This Story Fiction Or Non-Fiction? _____
_____

2. Could This Story Really Happen? _____
_____

3. What Is Your Favorite Part? Why? _____
_____
_____
_____

4. Do You Like The Story? _____ Why Or Why Not? _____
_____
_____

 What Would You Do If You Were In The Story
_____
_____
_____

Date.. / /

THIS BOOK MAKES ME FEEL

WHO ARE THE CHARACTERS?

1. _____
2. _____
3. _____
4. _____

IS THERE A PROBLEM?
Write About it

_____
_____
_____

WHAT HAPPENS AT THE...

BEGINNING OF THE STORY
Draw Or Write About it

MIDDLE OF THE STORY
Draw Or Write About it

ENDING OF THE STORY
Draw Or Write About it

Date.. / /

TODAY I READ ABOUT...
WRITE ABOUT IT, DRAW ABOUT IT, OR DO BOTH

Date.. / /

Whimsical Words

What New Words Will You Discover While Reading? Write Them In The Unicorn Below

Date.. / /

The Title Of My Book Is _____

The Author Is _____

Look At The Cover Of The Book What Do You Think This Book Is About? _____
_____
_____

1. Is This Story Fiction Or Non-Fiction? _____
_____

2. Could This Story Really Happen? _____
_____

3. What Is Your Favorite Part?   Why? _____
_____
_____
_____

4. Do You Like The Story? _____ Why Or Why Not? _____
_____
_____

☀ What Would You Do If You Were In The Story ☀
_____
_____
_____

Date.. / /

This Book Makes Me Feel

Who are the characters?

1. _____
2. _____
3. _____
4. _____

Is there a problem?
Write About it

_____
_____
_____
_____

What happens at the...

Beginning of the Story
Draw Or Write About it

Middle of the Story
Draw Or Write About it

Ending of the Story
Draw Or Write About it

Date.. / /

TODAY I READ ABOUT...
WRITE ABOUT IT, DRAW ABOUT IT, OR DO BOTH

_____

_____

_____

_____

_____

_____

Date.. / /

Whimsical Words

What New Words Will You Discover While Reading? Write Them In The Unicorn Below

Date.. / /

The Title Of My Book Is _____

The Author Is _____

Look At The Cover Of The Book What Do You Think This Book Is About? _____
_____
_____

1. Is This Story Fiction Or Non-Fiction? _____
_____

2. Could This Story Really Happen? _____
_____

3. What Is Your Favorite Part? Why? _____
_____
_____
_____

4. Do You Like The Story? _____ Why Or Why Not? _____
_____

What Would You Do If You Were In The Story
_____
_____
_____

Date.. / /

This book makes me feel

Who are the characters?

1. _____
2. _____
3. _____
4. _____

Is there a problem?
Write About it

_____
_____
_____
_____

What happens at the...

Beginning of the story
Draw Or Write About it

Middle of the story
Draw Or Write About it

Ending of the story
Draw Or Write About it

Date.. / /

TODAY I READ ABOUT...
WRITE ABOUT IT, DRAW ABOUT IT, OR DO BOTH

_____

_____
_____
_____
_____
_____
_____
_____

Date.. / /

Whimsical Words

What New Words Will You Discover While Reading? Write Them In The Unicorn Below

Date.. / /

The Title Of My Book Is _____

The Author Is _____

Look At The Cover Of The Book What Do You Think This Book Is About? _____
_____
_____

1. Is This Story Fiction Or Non-Fiction? _____
_____

2. Could This Story Really Happen? _____
_____

3. What Is Your Favorite Part? Why? _____
_____
_____

4. Do You Like The Story? _____ Why Or Why Not? _____
_____

What Would You Do If You Were In The Story
_____
_____
_____

Date.. / /

This book makes me feel

Who are the characters?

1. _____
2. _____
3. _____
4. _____

Is there a problem?
Write About it

What happens at the...

Beginning of the story
Draw Or Write About it

Middle of the story
Draw Or Write About it

Ending of the story
Draw Or Write About it

Date.. / /

TODAY I READ ABOUT...
WRITE ABOUT IT, DRAW ABOUT IT, OR DO BOTH

_____

_____

_____

_____

_____

_____

_____

Date.. / /

Whimsical Words

What New Words Will You Discover While Reading?
Write Them In The Unicorn Below

Date.. / /

The Title Of My Book Is _____

The Author Is _____

Look At The Cover Of The Book What Do You Think This Book Is About? _____
_____
_____

1. Is This Story Fiction Or Non-Fiction? _____
_____

2. Could This Story Really Happen? _____
_____

3. What Is Your Favorite Part? Why? _____
_____
_____
_____

4. Do You Like The Story? _____ Why Or Why Not? _____
_____
_____

 What Would You Do If You Were In The Story
_____
_____
_____

Date.. / /

This book makes me feel

Who are the characters?

1. _____
2. _____
3. _____
4. _____

Is there a problem?
Write About it

What happens at the...

Beginning of the story
Draw Or Write About it

Middle of the story
Draw Or Write About it

Ending of the story
Draw Or Write About it

Date.. / /

TODAY I READ ABOUT...
WRITE ABOUT IT, DRAW ABOUT IT, OR DO BOTH

_____

_____

_____

_____

_____

_____

_____

Date.. / /

Whimsical Words

What New Words Will You Discover While Reading? Write Them In The Unicorn Below

Date.. / /

The Title Of My Book Is _____

The Author Is _____

Look At The Cover Of The Book What Do You Think This Book Is About? _____
_____
_____

1. Is This Story Fiction Or Non-Fiction? _____
_____

2. Could This Story Really Happen? _____
_____

3. What Is Your Favorite Part? Why? _____
_____
_____
_____

4. Do You Like The Story? _____ Why Or Why Not? _____
_____

What Would You Do If You Were In The Story
_____
_____
_____

Date.. / /

THIS BOOK MAKES ME FEEL

WHO ARE THE CHARACTERS?

1. _____
2. _____
3. _____
4. _____

IS THERE A PROBLEM?
Write About it

_____
_____
_____
_____

WHAT HAPPENS AT THE...

BEGINNING OF THE STORY
Draw Or Write About it

MIDDLE OF THE STORY
Draw Or Write About it

ENDING OF THE STORY
Draw Or Write About it

Date.. / /

TODAY I READ ABOUT...
WRITE ABOUT IT, DRAW ABOUT IT, OR DO BOTH

_____

_____

_____

_____

_____

_____

_____

Date.. / /

Whimsical Words

What New Words Will You Discover While Reading?
Write Them In The Unicorn Below

Date.. / /

The Title Of My Book Is _____

The Author Is _____

Look At The Cover Of The Book What Do You Think This Book Is About? _____
_____
_____

1. Is This Story Fiction Or Non-Fiction? _____
_____

2. Could This Story Really Happen? _____
_____

3. What Is Your Favorite Part? Why? _____
_____
_____
_____

4. Do You Like The Story? _____ Why Or Why Not? _____
_____
_____

What Would You Do If You Were In The Story
_____
_____
_____

Date.. / /

THIS BOOK MAKES ME FEEL

WHO ARE THE CHARACTERS?

1. _____
2. _____
3. _____
4. _____

IS THERE A PROBLEM?
Write About it

_____
_____
_____
_____

WHAT HAPPENS AT THE...

BEGINNING OF THE STORY
Draw Or Write About it

MIDDLE OF THE STORY
Draw Or Write About it

ENDING OF THE STORY
Draw Or Write About it

Date.. / /

TODAY I READ ABOUT...
WRITE ABOUT IT, DRAW ABOUT IT, OR DO BOTH

_____

_____

_____

_____

_____

_____

_____

Date.. / /

Whimsical Words

What New Words Will You Discover While Reading?
Write Them In The Unicorn Below

Date.. / /

The Title Of My Book Is _____

The Author Is _____

Look At The Cover Of The Book What Do You Think This Book Is About? _____
_____
_____

1. Is This Story Fiction Or Non-Fiction? _____
_____

2. Could This Story Really Happen? _____
_____

3. What Is Your Favorite Part? Why? _____
_____
_____
_____

4. Do You Like The Story? _____ Why Or Why Not? _____
_____

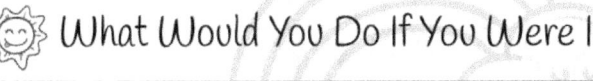 What Would You Do If You Were In The Story
_____
_____
_____

Date.. / /

THIS BOOK MAKES ME FEEL

WHO ARE THE CHARACTERS?

1. _____
2. _____
3. _____
4. _____

IS THERE A PROBLEM?
Write About it

_____
_____
_____

WHAT HAPPENS AT THE...

BEGINNING OF THE STORY
Draw Or Write About it

MIDDLE OF THE STORY
Draw Or Write About it

ENDING OF THE STORY
Draw Or Write About it

Date.. / /

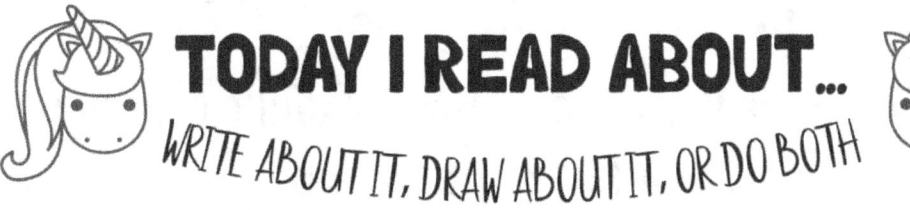

TODAY I READ ABOUT...
WRITE ABOUT IT, DRAW ABOUT IT, OR DO BOTH

_____

_____

_____

_____

_____

_____

_____

Date.. / /

Whimsical Words

What New Words Will You Discover While Reading? Write Them In The Unicorn Below

Date.. / /

The Title Of My Book Is _____

The Author Is _____

Look At The Cover Of The Book What Do You Think This Book Is About? _____
_____
_____

1. Is This Story Fiction Or Non-Fiction? _____
_____

2. Could This Story Really Happen? _____
_____

3. What Is Your Favorite Part? Why? _____
_____
_____
_____

4. Do You Like The Story? _____ Why Or Why Not? _____
_____
_____

 What Would You Do If You Were In The Story
_____
_____
_____

Date.. / /

This book makes me feel

Who are the characters?

1. _____
2. _____
3. _____
4. _____

Is there a problem?
Write About it

_____
_____
_____
_____

What happens at the...

Beginning of the story
Draw Or Write About it

Middle of the story
Draw Or Write About it

Ending of the story
Draw Or Write About it

Date.. / /

TODAY I READ ABOUT...

WRITE ABOUT IT, DRAW ABOUT IT, OR DO BOTH

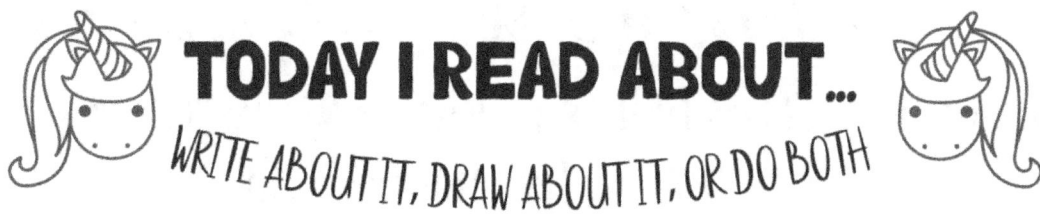

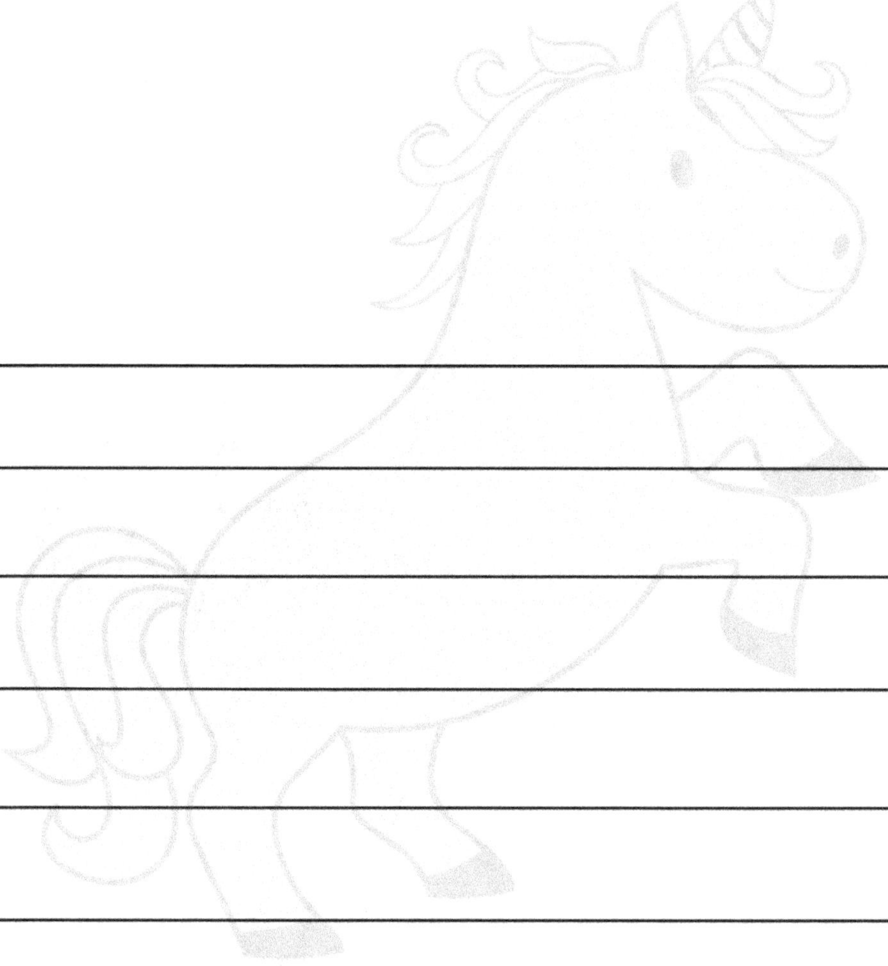

Date.. / /

Whimsical Words

What New Words Will You Discover While Reading?
Write Them In The Unicorn Below

Date.. / /

The Title Of My Book Is _____

The Author Is _____

Look At The Cover Of The Book What Do You Think This Book Is About? _____
_____
_____

1. Is This Story Fiction Or Non-Fiction? _____
_____

2. Could This Story Really Happen? _____
_____

3. What Is Your Favorite Part? Why? _____
_____
_____
_____

4. Do You Like The Story? _____ Why Or Why Not? _____
_____

 What Would You Do If You Were In The Story
_____
_____
_____

Date.. / /

This book makes me feel

Who are the characters?

1. _____
2. _____
3. _____
4. _____

Is there a problem?
Write About it

_____
_____
_____
_____

What happens at the...

Beginning of the story
Draw Or Write About it

Middle of the story
Draw Or Write About it

Ending of the story
Draw Or Write About it

Date.. / /

TODAY I READ ABOUT...
WRITE ABOUT IT, DRAW ABOUT IT, OR DO BOTH

Date.. / /

Whimsical Words

What New Words Will You Discover While Reading? Write Them In The Unicorn Below

Date.. / /

The Title Of My Book Is _____

The Author Is _____

Look At The Cover Of The Book What Do You Think This Book Is About? _____
_____
_____

1. Is This Story Fiction Or Non-Fiction? _____
_____

2. Could This Story Really Happen? _____
_____

3. What Is Your Favorite Part? Why? _____
_____
_____
_____

4. Do You Like The Story? _____ Why Or Why Not? _____
_____
_____

 What Would You Do If You Were In The Story
_____
_____
_____

Date.. / /

This Book Makes Me Feel

Who are the Characters?

1. _____
2. _____
3. _____
4. _____

Is There a Problem?
Write About it

_____
_____
_____

What Happens at the...

Beginning of the Story
Draw Or Write About it

Middle of the Story
Draw Or Write About it

Ending of the Story
Draw Or Write About it

Date.. / /

TODAY I READ ABOUT...
WRITE ABOUT IT, DRAW ABOUT IT, OR DO BOTH

_____

_____

_____

_____

_____

_____

_____

Date.. / /

Whimsical Words

What New Words Will You Discover While Reading?
Write Them In The Unicorn Below

Date.. / /

The Title Of My Book Is _____

The Author Is _____

Look At The Cover Of The Book What Do You Think This Book Is About? _____
_____
_____

1. Is This Story Fiction Or Non-Fiction? _____
_____

2. Could This Story Really Happen? _____
_____

3. What Is Your Favorite Part? Why? _____
_____
_____
_____

4. Do You Like The Story? _____ Why Or Why Not? _____
_____
_____

What Would You Do If You Were In The Story
_____
_____
_____

Date.. / /

This book makes me feel

Who are the characters?

1. _____
2. _____
3. _____
4. _____

Is there a problem?
Write About it

What happens at the...

Beginning of the story
Draw Or Write About it

Middle of the story
Draw Or Write About it

Ending of the story
Draw Or Write About it

Date.. / /

TODAY I READ ABOUT...
WRITE ABOUT IT, DRAW ABOUT IT, OR DO BOTH

_____

Date.. / /

Whimsical Words

What New Words Will You Discover While Reading?
Write Them In The Unicorn Below

Date.. / /

The Title Of My Book Is _____

The Author Is _____

Look At The Cover Of The Book What Do You Think This Book Is About? _____
_____
_____

1. Is This Story Fiction Or Non-Fiction? _____
_____

2. Could This Story Really Happen? _____
_____

3. What Is Your Favorite Part? Why? _____
_____
_____
_____

4. Do You Like The Story? _____ Why Or Why Not? _____
_____
_____

 What Would You Do If You Were In The Story
_____
_____
_____

Date.. / /

THIS BOOK MAKES ME FEEL

WHO ARE THE CHARACTERS?

1. _____
2. _____
3. _____
4. _____

IS THERE A PROBLEM?
Write About it

_____
_____
_____
_____

WHAT HAPPENS AT THE...

BEGINNING OF THE STORY
Draw Or Write About it

MIDDLE OF THE STORY
Draw Or Write About it

ENDING OF THE STORY
Draw Or Write About it

Date.. / /

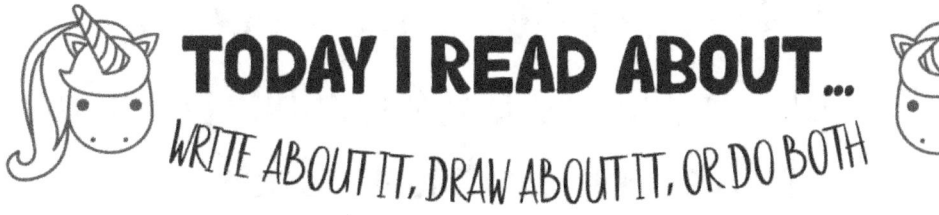

TODAY I READ ABOUT...
WRITE ABOUT IT, DRAW ABOUT IT, OR DO BOTH

_____

_____

_____

_____

_____

_____

_____

Date.. / /

Whimsical Words

What New Words Will You Discover While Reading? Write Them In The Unicorn Below

Date.. / /

The Title Of My Book Is _____

The Author Is _____

Look At The Cover Of The Book What Do You Think This Book Is About? _____
_____
_____

1. Is This Story Fiction Or Non-Fiction? _____
_____

2. Could This Story Really Happen? _____
_____

3. What Is Your Favorite Part? Why? _____
_____
_____
_____

4. Do You Like The Story? _____ Why Or Why Not? _____
_____
_____

What Would You Do If You Were In The Story
_____
_____
_____

Date.. / /

THIS BOOK MAKES ME FEEL

WHO ARE THE CHARACTERS?

1. _____
2. _____
3. _____
4. _____

IS THERE A PROBLEM?
Write About it

_____
_____
_____
_____

WHAT HAPPENS AT THE...

BEGINNING OF THE STORY
Draw Or Write About it

MIDDLE OF THE STORY
Draw Or Write About it

ENDING OF THE STORY
Draw Or Write About it

Date.. / /

TODAY I READ ABOUT...
WRITE ABOUT IT, DRAW ABOUT IT, OR DO BOTH

_____

_____

_____

_____

_____

_____

_____

Date.. / /

Whimsical Words

What New Words Will You Discover While Reading?
Write Them In The Unicorn Below

Date.. / /

The Title Of My Book Is _____

The Author Is _____

Look At The Cover Of The Book What Do You Think This Book Is About? _____
_____
_____

1. Is This Story Fiction Or Non-Fiction? _____
_____

2. Could This Story Really Happen? _____
_____

3. What Is Your Favorite Part? Why? _____
_____
_____
_____

4. Do You Like The Story? _____ Why Or Why Not? _____
_____
_____

What Would You Do If You Were In The Story
_____
_____
_____

Date.. / /

This book makes me feel

Who are the characters?

1. _____
2. _____
3. _____
4. _____

Is there a problem?
Write About it

What happens at the...

Beginning of the story
Draw Or Write About it

Middle of the story
Draw Or Write About it

Ending of the story
Draw Or Write About it

Date.. / /

TODAY I READ ABOUT...
WRITE ABOUT IT, DRAW ABOUT IT, OR DO BOTH

_____
_____

_____

_____

_____

_____

_____

_____

Date.. / /

Whimsical Words

What New Words Will You Discover While Reading?
Write Them In The Unicorn Below

Date.. / /

The Title Of My Book Is _____

The Author Is _____

Look At The Cover Of The Book What Do You Think This Book Is About? _____
_____
_____

1. Is This Story Fiction Or Non-Fiction? _____
_____

2. Could This Story Really Happen? _____
_____

3. What Is Your Favorite Part? Why? _____
_____
_____
_____

4. Do You Like The Story? _____ Why Or Why Not? _____
_____
_____

 What Would You Do If You Were In The Story
_____
_____
_____

Date.. / /

THIS BOOK MAKES ME FEEL

WHO ARE THE CHARACTERS?

1. _____
2. _____
3. _____
4. _____

IS THERE A PROBLEM?
Write About it

_____
_____
_____
_____

WHAT HAPPENS AT THE...

BEGINNING OF THE STORY
Draw Or Write About it

MIDDLE OF THE STORY
Draw Or Write About it

ENDING OF THE STORY
Draw Or Write About it

Date.. / /

TODAY I READ ABOUT...
WRITE ABOUT IT, DRAW ABOUT IT, OR DO BOTH

_____
_____

_____

_____

_____

_____

_____

_____

Date.. / /

Whimsical Words

What New Words Will You Discover While Reading? Write Them In The Unicorn Below

Date.. / /

The Title Of My Book Is _____

The Author Is _____

Look At The Cover Of The Book What Do You Think This Book Is About? _____
_____
_____

1. Is This Story Fiction Or Non-Fiction? _____
_____

2. Could This Story Really Happen? _____
_____

3. What Is Your Favorite Part? Why? _____
_____
_____
_____

4. Do You Like The Story? _____ Why Or Why Not? _____
_____
_____

☀ What Would You Do If You Were In The Story ☀
_____
_____
_____

Date.. / /

THIS BOOK MAKES ME FEEL

WHO ARE THE CHARACTERS?

1. _____
2. _____
3. _____
4. _____

IS THERE A PROBLEM?
Write About it

WHAT HAPPENS AT THE...

BEGINNING OF THE STORY
Draw Or Write About it

MIDDLE OF THE STORY
Draw Or Write About it

ENDING OF THE STORY
Draw Or Write About it

Date.. / /

TODAY I READ ABOUT...
WRITE ABOUT IT, DRAW ABOUT IT, OR DO BOTH

_____

_____
_____
_____
_____
_____
_____

Date.. / /

Whimsical Words

What New Words Will You Discover While Reading?
Write Them In The Unicorn Below

Date.. / /

The Title Of My Book Is _____

The Author Is _____

Look At The Cover Of The Book What Do You Think This Book Is About? _____
_____
_____

1. Is This Story Fiction Or Non-Fiction? _____
_____

2. Could This Story Really Happen? _____
_____

3. What Is Your Favorite Part? Why? _____
_____
_____

4. Do You Like The Story? _____ Why Or Why Not? _____
_____

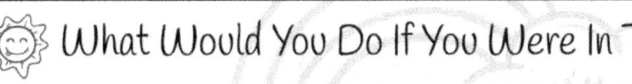 What Would You Do If You Were In The Story
_____
_____
_____

Date.. / /

THIS BOOK MAKES ME FEEL

WHO ARE THE CHARACTERS?

1. _____
2. _____
3. _____
4. _____

IS THERE A PROBLEM?
Write About it

WHAT HAPPENS AT THE...

BEGINNING OF THE STORY
Draw Or Write About it

MIDDLE OF THE STORY
Draw Or Write About it

ENDING OF THE STORY
Draw Or Write About it

Date.. / /

TODAY I READ ABOUT...
WRITE ABOUT IT, DRAW ABOUT IT, OR DO BOTH

Date.. / /

Whimsical Words

What New Words Will You Discover While Reading?
Write Them In The Unicorn Below

Date.. / /

The Title Of My Book Is _____

The Author Is _____

Look At The Cover Of The Book What Do You Think This Book Is About? _____
_____
_____

1. Is This Story Fiction Or Non-Fiction? _____
_____

2. Could This Story Really Happen? _____
_____

3. What Is Your Favorite Part? Why? _____
_____
_____
_____

4. Do You Like The Story? _____ Why Or Why Not? _____
_____

What Would You Do If You Were In The Story
_____
_____
_____

Date.. / /

This book makes me feel

Who are the characters?

1. _____
2. _____
3. _____
4. _____

Is there a problem?
Write About it

_____
_____
_____
_____

What happens at the...

Beginning of the story
Draw Or Write About it

Middle of the story
Draw Or Write About it

Ending of the story
Draw Or Write About it

Date.. / /

TODAY I READ ABOUT...
WRITE ABOUT IT, DRAW ABOUT IT, OR DO BOTH

_____

_____
_____
_____
_____
_____
_____
_____

www.ingramcontent.com/pod-product-compliance
Lightning Source LLC
Chambersburg PA
CBHW081620100526
44590CB00021B/3528